Desserts Grow on Stevia Plants

A Stevia-Friendly Dessert Cookbook for Guilt-Free Indulgence

BY - Zoe Moore

Copyright 2022 by Zoe Moore

Copyright Notes

I've spent a lifetime in the kitchen, and all the knowledge I've accumulated from that hasn't come without its fair share of burns and disasters. Fortunately, I'm a lot wiser from it all and am now in a place where I can share my knowledge and skills with you. However, that doesn't mean anyone can use my content for any purpose they please. This book has been copyrighted as a way to protect my story, knowledge, and recipes, so I can continue sharing them with others into the future.

Do not make any print or electronic reproductions, sell, re-publish, or distribute this book in parts or as a whole unless you have express written consent from me or my team.

This is a condensed version of the copyright license, but it's everything you need to know in a nutshell. Please help protect my life's work and all the burns and melted spatulas I have accumulated in order to publish this book.

Table of Contents

Introduction 5

(1) Peanut Butter Mousse 7

(2) Stevia Lemon Bars 9

(3) Stevia Pumpkin Pie 12

(4) Stevia Meringue Cookies 15

(5) Hazelnut Balls with Stevia 17

(6) Vanilla Ice Cream with Stevia 19

(7) Stevia Lemon Muffins 21

(8) Stevia Raspberry Mousse 24

(9) Lemon Blueberry Pound Cake 26

(10) Stevia Apple Crumble 29

(11) Stevia Peanut Butter Mug Cake 31

(12) Stevia Banana Bread 33

(13) Pumpkin Chocolate Bites 35

(14) Stevia Brownies 37

(15) Snack Bars with Stevia 40

(16) Stevia Frosting 42

(17) Stevia Pecan Pie 44

(18) Stevia Coconut Brownies 46

(19) Stevia Brownies 48

(20) Stevia Hot Chocolate 50

(21) No Bake Cookies 52

(22) Stevia Chocolate Bars 54

(23) Chocolate Zucchini Bread Sweetened with Stevia 56

(24) Vanilla Creme Pudding with Stevia 59

(25) Coated Nuts with Stevia 61

(26) Stevia Royal Icing 63

(27) Stevia Lemonade 65

(28) Stevia Simple Syrup 67

(29) Stevia Cookie Dough 69

(30) Stevia Lemon Cookies 71

About the Author 73

Author's Afterthoughts 74

Introduction

We know you're on a diet, but please stop torturing yourself with all those terrible low-calorie desserts you have. Right now! Making your own stevia-friendly desserts might not have occurred to you earlier, but it doesn't mean you can't start now! What'd you get this cookbook for then?

Amateur or pro home-cooks, we've included the easiest and most delicious guilt-free desserts in our cookbook so that you never have to punish your body for being on a diet with those disgusting diet treats you buy sometimes. The recipes in your hands have been carefully developed and tested by our entire team over the course of a year to ensure there's no weird effect from all the stevia. The fact that you're holding the cookbook right now means we've succeeded in our mission.

"Desserts Grow on Stevia Plants" comes with lots of your favorite dessert recipes like Brownies, Lemon Bars and Pecan Pie. To make things even more interesting, though, we've decided to add lots of new recipes that you would've never thought to make with stevia, too; for example, Meringue Cookies, Apple Crumble and Vanilla Creme Pudding. Since it's almost time for dessert, can you please choose a recipe, so we can get started? Good luck!

xxxxxxxxxxxxxxxxxxxxxxxxxxxxxxxxxxxxxxxxxxx

(1) Peanut Butter Mousse

This mousse is an elegant and presentable dessert, which is easy to prepare. The peanut butter adds a dose of flavor and creaminess, making your dessert heaven for the taste buds.

Duration: 1 hour 10 minutes

Serving Size: 3

List of Ingredients:

- 2 cups heavy cream
- 2 scoops vanilla collagen powder
- 1 cup peanut butter
- ½ cup powdered stevia
- 2 tbsp. warm water
- 2 tsp. gelatin

xxxxxxxxxxxxxxxxxxxxxxxxxxxxxxxxxxxxxxxxxxxx

How to Cook:

Beat the heavy cream on high continuously till soft peaks form.

Add the vanilla collagen powder and powdered stevia gradually. Beat again until stiff peaks.

Add the peanut butter and fold with a spatula.

Mix the warm water and gelatin until dissolved.

Add into the whipped cream and beat on low. Serve in small bowls and chill for at least 1 hour.

(2) Stevia Lemon Bars

When you prefer fresh and creamy desserts to satisfy your cravings, these lemon bars are one excellent option. The fresh citrus flavor uplifts the dessert, while the stevia adds extra sweetness without raising the calories.

Duration: 3 hours 10 minutes

Serving Size: 12

List of Ingredients:

- 1 cup gluten-free baking flour
- 2 tbsp. coconut sugar
- 1/3 cup coconut oil
- 1 tbsp. milk
- 1 tsp. lemon juice
- ¼ tsp. salt

Filling:

- 2 eggs, room temperature
- 3 cups Greek yogurt
- 1 tsp. lemon extract
- 1/8 cup lemon juice
- 2 tsp. powdered stevia
- 1 tsp. tapioca flour
- 2 tbsp. lemon zest for topping

xxxxxxxxxxxxxxxxxxxxxxxxxxxxxxxxxxxxxxxxxxxxx

How to Cook:

Preheat the oven to 350 degrees F.

Line a baking pan with paper and grease.

Using the mixer, combine the coconut sugar, lemon juice, coconut oil, milk and salt.

Add the gluten-free baking flour and mix.

Add the dough into a baking pan and flatten it.

Bake for 15 minutes. Remove and cool for 20 minutes.

Combine all the ingredients for the filling, leaving out the lemon zest.

Preheat the oven to 325 degrees F.

Add the filling over the crust.

Bake for 35 minutes.

Remove and cool for 2 hours before serving. Sprinkle with the lemon zest and serve.

(3) Stevia Pumpkin Pie

Whenever you want to enjoy a comforting pumpkin pie without the feeling of guilt, this is your ultimate recipe. It will taste the same while having fewer calories than the one packed with refined sugar.

Duration: 55 minutes

Serving Size: 8

List of Ingredients:

- 4 eggs
- 1 cup stevia
- 1 tsp. cinnamon
- 1 tbsp. flour
- ½ tsp. salt
- 1 tsp. cloves
- ¼ tsp. ginger
- 3 tbsp. butter, melted
- 1 cup pumpkin
- 1 ½ cups milk
- 1 9-inch unbaked pie crust

xxxxxxxxxxxxxxxxxxxxxxxxxxxxxxxxxxxxxxxxxxxxxx

How to Cook:

Beat the eggs and set them aside.

Mix the stevia, cinnamon, flour, cloves, salt and ginger.

Add the mixture to the beaten eggs.

Add the pumpkin and butter and stir well.

Add the milk and mix until incorporated.

Transfer onto the pie crust.

Bake for 15 minutes at 450 degrees F.

Reduce to 350 degrees F and bake for half an hour.

(4) Stevia Meringue Cookies

Meringue cookies are an elegant and sophisticated dessert, perfect for any occasion. This recipe will show you how to switch the sugar with stevia but still keep the original flavor and aesthetics.

Duration: 2 hours 10 minutes

Serving Size: 6

List of Ingredients:

- 5 egg whites
- ¾ tsp. stevia
- ¼ tsp. + ⅛ tsp. cream of tartar

xxxxxxxxxxxxxxxxxxxxxxxxxxxxxxxxxxxxxxxxxxxx

How to Cook:

Preheat the oven to 215 degrees F.

Prepare 2 baking sheets with parchment paper.

Whisk the cream of tartar and egg whites.

Gradually add the stevia while mixing.

When you have stiff peaks, spoon the mixture onto the baking sheets.

Bake for 2 hours.

(5) Hazelnut Balls with Stevia

When you are looking for a special occasion dessert, these hazelnut balls are your best option. The decadent center and crunchy outside create a perfect contrast, while the stevia still keeps the calories to a minimum.

Duration: 10 minutes

Serving Size: 12

List of Ingredients:

- ½ cup homemade Nutella (hazelnut butter, cocoa and sweetener of your choice)
- 12 hazelnuts
- ¼ cup hazelnuts, chopped
- 2 oz. sugar free chocolate bar

xxxxxxxxxxxxxxxxxxxxxxxxxxxxxxxxxxxxxxxxxxxxx

How to Cook:

Toast the hazelnuts until lightly brown. Cool and peel.

Take the Nutella. Flatten the mixture over parchment paper.

Shape the mixture into balls.

Chill in the fridge.

Melt the chocolate bar and add 1 cup of the hazelnuts.

Dip the balls in the chocolate. Chill and serve.

(6) Vanilla Ice Cream with Stevia

If you are craving creamy and delicious ice cream, this is the right recipe for you. The decadent icy dessert will tingle your taste buds, and you will want it more. No need to hesitate as this is low in calories.

Duration: 4 hours 35 minutes

Serving Size: 8

List of Ingredients:

- 1 cup whole full-fat milk
- 1 tbsp. stevia powder
- 1 tsp. vanilla extract
- 2 cups heavy cream
- Pinch of salt

xxxxxxxxxxxxxxxxxxxxxxxxxxxxxxxxxxxxxxxxxxxx

How to Cook:

Beat the milk with the hand mixer on low speed, together with the salt and stevia powder. Mix until dissolved.

Add the vanilla extract and heavy cream. Chill in the fridge for 2 hours.

Churn the stevia ice cream mixture in your ice cream maker for 35 minutes or until creamy and soft. Freeze for more 2 hours and serve.

(7) Stevia Lemon Muffins

When you crave fluffy muffins with a lemon flavor, these muffins will exceed your expectations. They are easy to prepare and will amaze your guests for sure.

Duration: 40 minutes

Serving Size: 5

List of Ingredients:

- 2 tbsp. whole milk
- 3 large eggs
- 1 tbsp. fresh lemon juice
- ¼ cup unsalted butter, melted and slightly cooled
- 1 tsp. stevia glycerite
- ¼ tsp. sea salt
- 1 tbsp. lemon zest
- ¼ cup coconut flour
- ¼ tsp. baking soda
- 1 tbsp. poppy seeds

xxxxxxxxxxxxxxxxxxxxxxxxxxxxxxxxxxxxxxxxxxxxx

How to Cook:

Preheat the oven to 350 degrees F.

Grease a muffin pan.

Whisk the milk, eggs, butter, lemon juice, salt and stevia glycerite.

Add the coconut flour and lemon zest. Mix until combined and smooth.

Add the baking soda and stir well.

Fold in the poppy seeds with the help of your spatula.

Pour into the pan.

Bake for 15 minutes and cool before removing.

(8) Stevia Raspberry Mousse

When you are craving a creamy and decadent sweet dessert, this raspberry mousse will suit your taste. The fluffy berry-enriched mousse will enhance every sweet-toothed individual. Decorate with a few fresh raspberries for the ultimate presentation.

Duration: 45 minutes

Serving Size: 6

List of Ingredients:

- 1 tbsp. gelatin
- 2 tbsp. cold water
- 3 tbsp. boiling water
- 2 cups raspberries
- 1 tsp. vanilla extract
- ⅛ tsp. stevia
- 1 ½ cups heavy cream
- ⅓ cup low carb sugar substitute

xxxxxxxxxxxxxxxxxxxxxxxxxxxxxxxxxxxxxxxxxxxxx

How to Cook:

Mix the gelatin with the cold water. Leave for a minute and add the boiling water. Mix well until dissolved and let it cool down.

Cook the stevia and raspberries over medium-low heat. Let the mixture cool and run through a strainer to remove the seeds.

Add the gelatin and combine.

Whip the heavy cream together with the vanilla extract and sugar substitute.

(9) Lemon Blueberry Pound Cake

A fluffy and spongy pound cake is a perfect combination with a cup of coffee. This pound cake is enhanced with a citrus vibe and berry flavor, the ideal variety for sweet-toothed foodies.

Duration:1 hour 30 minutes

Serving Size: 16

List of Ingredients:

- 1 cup softened butter
- 8 oz. cream cheese
- 1 cup low carb sugar substitute
- 2 tbsp. coconut flour
- ½ tsp. stevia powder
- 2 tsp. lemon extract
- 2 tsp. vanilla extract
- 10 eggs
- 2 tsp. baking powder
- 2 ¼ cups almond flour
- ½ cup coconut flour
- 2 cups blueberries

Glaze

- 2-3 tbsp. lemon juice
- ½ cup confectioners sweetener

xxxxxxxxxxxxxxxxxxxxxxxxxxxxxxxxxxxxxxxxx

How to Cook:

Beat the cream cheese, butter and sugar substitute.

Add the extracts and eggs and mix.

Combine 2 tablespoons of the coconut flour, the almond flour, stevia powder and baking powder in a second bowl.

Add the flour mixture to the egg mixture gradually.

Sprinkle the blueberries with ½ cup of the coconut flour and add them over the mixture.

Bake in a grease Bundt pan and bake for 1 hour and 15 minutes at 325 degrees F or until a toothpick comes out clean.

Mix all the glaze ingredients and pour over the cake once cooled down.

(10) Stevia Apple Crumble

If apple crumble is your favorite comfort food, don't miss this fantastic recipe. It will show you exactly how to switch the sugar with stevia to enjoy a healthy dessert.

Duration: 50 minutes

Serving Size: 6

List of Ingredients:

- 5 apples
- 1 unsalted butter stick
- 1/3 cup water
- ¾ cup flour
- 2 tbsp. stevia
- 2 tbsp. stevia light brown sugar
- 1 tbsp. cinnamon

xxxxxxxxxxxxxxxxxxxxxxxxxxxxxxxxxxxxxxxxxxxx

How to Cook:

Preheat your oven to 350 degrees F

Peel, core and slice the apples. Add them to a greased baking dish.

Pour the water.

Sprinkle the cinnamon.

In a mixing bowl, combine the stevia, stevia light brown sugar, flour and butter.

Spread the mixture over the apples in the dish. Bake for 40 minutes.

(11) Stevia Peanut Butter Mug Cake

When you are feeling too tired to make a dessert that satisfies your sweet cravings, this recipe is here to save you. The addition of the peanut butter adds creaminess and extra flavor, while the whole cake takes less than 10 minutes to prepare.

Duration: 6 minutes

Serving Size: 1

List of Ingredients:

- ¼ cup creamy natural peanut butter
- 1 large egg
- ½ tsp. stevia liquid sweetener
- ¼ tsp. baking soda

xxxxxxxxxxxxxxxxxxxxxxxxxxxxxxxxxxxxxxxxxxxxx

How to Cook:

In a microwave-safe mug, add the egg and peanut butter. Mix well.

Add the baking soda and stevia liquid sweetener and combine.

Microwave for half a minute. Return for 10 more seconds until the edges are set.

(12) Stevia Banana Bread

Banana bread is an excellent choice for snack time. Even though the natural sweetness of banana is enough, you can add stevia to get a tasty dessert. This fantastic recipe will show you how to replace the sugar with stevia, step by step.

Duration: 1 hour 15 minutes

Serving Size: 12

List of Ingredients:

- ½ cup canola oil
- ¾ cup stevia
- 3 ripe bananas, sliced
- 2 eggs
- 1 tsp. baking soda
- 1 tsp. vanilla extract
- 2 cups all-purpose flour
- 1 tsp. salt
- 3 tbsp. sour cream
- Cooking spray

xxxxxxxxxxxxxxxxxxxxxxxxxxxxxxxxxxxxxxxxxxxxx

How to Cook:

Preheat the oven to 350 degrees F.

Sift the salt, baking soda and all-purpose flour.

Beat the eggs, canola oil and stevia with the mixer. Beat on low until thoroughly combined.

Add the bananas and beat them until you break them down into small pieces.

Add the sifted mixture and mix.

Bring in the sour cream and vanilla extract and beat for half a minute.

Grease and flour a baking pan. Add the mixture and bake for 1 hour.

(13) Pumpkin Chocolate Bites

These pumpkin bites with extra chocolate are a decadent and rich dessert, ready to be consumed anytime you want. The gooey texture and rich flavor will amaze every dessert lover out there.

Duration: 20 minutes

Serving Size: 20

List of Ingredients:

- ½ cup peanut butter
- 3 tbsp. defatted peanut butter powder
- 2 tbsp. coconut oil, extra if needed
- 4 tbsp. stevia
- 1 tsp. vanilla extract
- ¼ cup coconut flour
- 2 tbsp. pumpkin puree
- 1 tsp. pumpkin spice seasoning
- 1 tbsp. stevia-sweetened chocolate chips
- 1 cup sugar-free chocolate chips
- 1 tbsp. coconut oil

xxxxxxxxxxxxxxxxxxxxxxxxxxxxxxxxxxxxxxxxxxxxx

How to Cook:

Mix all the ingredients with the mixer, leaving the chocolate chips and 1 tablespoon of the coconut oil.

Work until you have a dough. If it is too crumbly, add more coconut oil.

Chill in the fridge for 10 minutes. Remove and shape the dough into balls.

Melt the chocolate chips with coconut oil in the microwave.

Dip the balls into the chocolate.

Child in the freezer until hardened.

(14) Stevia Brownies

If you crave chewy and delicious brownies at this moment, this recipe is your best choice. The brownies are decadent and highly delicious, while the preparation process is too easy and fast.

Duration: 40 minutes

Serving Size: 16

List of Ingredients:

- ½ cup canola oil
- ½ cup unsweetened applesauce
- 1 cup powdered stevia extract
- 3 eggs
- ¾ cup all-purpose flour
- 2 tsp. vanilla
- ½ tsp. baking powder
- 1/3 cup cocoa powder
- 1 cup sugar-free chocolate chip cookies, divided

xxxxxxxxxxxxxxxxxxxxxxxxxxxxxxxxxxxxxxxxxx

How to Cook:

Preheat the oven to 350 degrees F. Line your baking dish with parchment paper.

Mix the baking powder, cocoa powder and all-purpose flour.

Beat the applesauce, canola oil, eggs, powdered stevia extract and vanilla on low.

Add the flour mixture gradually while beating.

Fold in ½ cup of the chocolate chip cookies.

Transfer your brownie mixture to the baking dish and top with the remaining chocolate chip cookies.

Bake for 25 to 28 minutes or until a toothpick comes out with fudgy crumbs.

Cool and cut.

(15) Snack Bars with Stevia

If you want to make a healthy snack choice, prepare a large batch of these bars and keep them in the fridge. They make meal prepping effortless and fast, so you don't have to worry about the choices.

Duration: 30 minutes

Serving Size: 12

List of Ingredients:

- ½ cup coconut oil
- ¼ cup cocoa powder
- 1/8 tsp. vanilla liquid stevia
- ¼ tsp. vanilla extract
- Pinch of salt

xxxxxxxxxxxxxxxxxxxxxxxxxxxxxxxxxxxxxxxxxxxxx

How to Cook:

Line a cake pan with parchment paper.

Mix all the ingredients in a microwave-safe bowl. Microwave for 20 to 30 seconds or until melted.

Mix well and transfer into the pan.

Set in the freezer for half an hour.

Break with hands and serve.

(16) Stevia Frosting

This is your best recipe to follow when you want to enhance your stevia desserts with fluffy frosting. The frosting is neutral and can match any dessert of your choice. Feel free to pair it with any of the recipes in this cookbook.

Duration: 10 minutes

Serving Size: 12

List of Ingredients:

- 8 oz. cream cheese
- ¼ cup softened unsalted butter
- 2 tbsp. Greek yogurt, extra if needed
- 1 tsp. stevia
- 1 tsp. vanilla extract

xxxxxxxxxxxxxxxxxxxxxxxxxxxxxxxxxxxxxxxxxxxxx

How to Cook:

Beat the butter and cream cheese with a paddle attachment.

Mix in Greek yogurt.

Mix in the vanilla extract and stevia for a minute at medium speed.

Whip until you reach the desired thickness. If too thick, mix in some more Greek yogurt.

(17) Stevia Pecan Pie

This recipe is rich with flavor and texture for the ultimate gourmet experience. You don't have to waste much time preparing it. Follow the recipe for the ultimate dessert that suits your taste.

Duration: 3 hours 10 minutes

Serving Size: 12

List of Ingredients:

- 1 frozen pie crust
- 5 tsp. stevia
- 3 eggs
- 1 cup pure maple syrup
- 1 cup pecans, halved
- 1 tsp. vanilla
- 1/3 cup coconut oil, melted

xxxxxxxxxxxxxxxxxxxxxxxxxxxxxxxxxxxxxxxxxxxxx

How to Cook:

Preheat the oven to 350 degrees F.

Mix the stevia and eggs.

Add in the vanilla, coconut oil, maple syrup and pecans. Mix well to combine.

Transfer into the pie crust and bake it for 45 minutes or until golden brown. Let it cool before slicing.

(18) Stevia Coconut Brownies

These coconut brownies are perfect for those days when you crave rich and flavorful desserts. They are so easy to prepare when you follow our detailed instructions.

Duration: 40 minutes

Serving Size: 16

List of Ingredients:

- 15 oz. black beans, rinsed and drained
- 2 tbsp. cocoa powder
- ½ cup honey
- ½ cup oats
- 1 tsp. stevia
- 1 cup unsweetened shredded coconut
- ¼ cup coconut oil
- 1 tbsp. vanilla
- ½ tsp. baking powder
- 10 oz. dark chocolate chips
- 1 tsp. almond extract

xxxxxxxxxxxxxxxxxxxxxxxxxxxxxxxxxxxxxxxxxxxxx

How to Cook:

Preheat the oven to 350 degrees F.

Puree the black beans in the food processor.

Add the rest of the ingredients, leaving out the dark chocolate chips.

Process until smooth. Fold in the chocolate chips.

Transfer in a greased baking dish. Bake for 25 to 30 minutes.

(19) Stevia Brownies

While you can't have enough brownies, this version is one of the must-have brownies to fit in your collection. The chewy and gooey center contributes to a decadent flavor, while you don't have to worry about adding calories to your diet.

Duration: 40 minutes

Serving Size: 16

List of Ingredients:

- 5 oz. dark chocolate
- 7 oz. unsalted butter
- ¼ cup stevia
- Pinch of salt
- 1 tsp. vanilla essence
- 4 eggs
- 5 oz. almond flour

xxxxxxxxxxxxxxxxxxxxxxxxxxxxxxxxxxxxxxxxxxxxx

How to Cook:

Preheat the oven to 350 degrees F. Line an aligned sheet with paper and grease it.

Melt the dark chocolate and butter over low heat. Add the salt, vanilla essence and stevia.

Whisk in the eggs one by one.

Mix in the almond flour.

Transfer into the sheet.

Bake for 25 minutes and cool before slicing.

(20) Stevia Hot Chocolate

If you love to enjoy a good book along with a cup of hot chocolate, this recipe will soon become your favorite. The sweetness from the stevia gives it a decadent flavor while still making a low-calorie treat.

Duration: 5 minutes

Serving Size: 1

List of Ingredients:

- 8 oz. milk
- 1/8 tsp. stevia powder
- 2 tsp. organic cocoa powder

xxxxxxxxxxxxxxxxxxxxxxxxxxxxxxxxxxxxxxxxxxxxx

How to Cook:

Place the milk in a pot over medium heat. When it starts to boil, remove it.

Add the other ingredients and mix well until combined. Serve warm.

(21) No Bake Cookies

If you crave something sweet and don't have enough time, these cookies are your go-to recipe. Whip them up within a short time and enjoy them on a busy weekday.

Duration: 15 minutes

Serving Size: 10

List of Ingredients:

- 2 tbsp. butter, melted
- 2/3 cup all-natural peanut butter
- 4 drops vanilla stevia
- 1 cup unsweetened shredded coconut

xxxxxxxxxxxxxxxxxxxxxxxxxxxxxxxxxxxxxxxxxxxx

How to Cook:

Let the butter cool a little.

Add the peanut butter and mix well.

Add the shredded coconut and vanilla stevia and blend together.

Spoon into a sheet pan and place it in the freezer for 10 minutes.

(22) Stevia Chocolate Bars

These chocolate bars are the perfect snack for any day of the week. Let's try them today!

Duration: 2 hours 30 minutes

Serving Size: 5

List of Ingredients:

- ⅓ cup coconut cream
- 1 cup unsweetened shredded coconut
- ½ tsp. powdered stevia
- 2 tbsp. unsweetened cocoa powder
- 4 tbsp. coconut oil
- 1 tsp. vanilla extract

xxxxxxxxxxxxxxxxxxxxxxxxxxxxxxxxxxxxxxxxxxxxx

How to Cook:

Combine the coconut cream, shredded coconut, half of the stevia, and half of the vanilla extract.

Place onto paper lie down and shape flat into a one-inch thick rectangle.

Freeze for 2 hours.

Cut into 5 bars.

Melt the coconut oil and add the cocoa powder, remaining vanilla extract and remaining stevia.

Heat on low heat and mix until combined.

Let the chocolate cool a little at room temperature before you cover the bars in it. Return them on a plate and set them in the fridge to harden.

(23) Chocolate Zucchini Bread Sweetened with Stevia

This recipe is fluffy, decadent and rich in flavor. Whether you are looking for a healthy and tasty snack or a yummy cake to go with your coffee, this is a good choice to stick with.

Duration: 55 minutes

Serving Size: 12

List of Ingredients:

- ½ cup sugar-free chocolate chips
- 2 cups zucchini, shredded

Dry Ingredients:

- ½ cup coconut flour
- ¼ tsp. salt
- 1 tsp. baking powder
- 1 tsp. baking soda
- ½ tsp. ground cinnamon
- ½ cup unsweetened cocoa powder
- ½ cup stevia

Wet Ingredients:

- 4 large eggs
- ¼ cup coconut oil
- 1 tsp. vanilla extract

xxxxxxxxxxxxxxxxxxxxxxxxxxxxxxxxxxxxxxxxxxxxx

How to Cook:

Mix the dry ingredients in a bowl.

Add in the wet ingredients and stir until combined.

Add the chocolate chips and zucchini and gently fold them in.

Transfer the mixture to a loaf pan arranged with paper.

Bake at 350 degrees F for 45 to 55 minutes. Cool before removing.

(24) Vanilla Creme Pudding with Stevia

This vanilla creme pudding is a presentable dessert that you can whip up in no time. It is a good choice if you get those urgent cravings or have some unplanned visitors. Either way, you are guaranteed full enjoyment.

Duration: 12 minutes

Serving Size: 4

List of Ingredients:

- 1 can refrigerated full-fat coconut milk
- 10 drops liquid stevia
- 1 tsp. vanilla extract
- ½ cup berries of your choice
- 90 g walnuts, chopped

xxxxxxxxxxxxxxxxxxxxxxxxxxxxxxxxxxxxxxxxxxxxx

How to Cook:

Mix the coconut milk, vanilla extract and liquid stevia with a whisk attachment for half a minute. Set aside.

Mix the walnuts and berries in a small bowl and set aside.

Divide the pudding into 4 bowls. Divide the walnut mixture on top.

(25) Coated Nuts with Stevia

These coated nuts are a perfect snack or appetizer with a good drink. If you wish to avoid the extra calories, they will suit your needs.

Duration: 15 minutes

Serving Size: 4

List of Ingredients:

- 4 tbsp. stevia
- 1 ½ tsp. vanilla extract
- 2 ½ tbsp. water
- ½ tsp. salt
- 1 ¼ cups nuts

xxxxxxxxxxxxxxxxxxxxxxxxxxxxxxxxxxxxxxxxxxxxxx

How to Cook:

Line a baking sheet with paper.

In a small pot, mix the vanilla extract, water, salt and stevia. Cook on medium heat while stirring.

When it comes to boil, add the nuts. Mix until caramelized

Remove from the heat and carefully place over the baking sheet.

Cool down and serve.

(26) Stevia Royal Icing

If you want to enhance your cookies with low-calorie icing, this recipe will help you. It reveals the whole process and tips and tricks on preparing the best stevia royal icing.

Duration: 20 minutes

Serving Size: 12

List of Ingredients:

- 3 tsp. meringue powder
- 3 cups stevia baking blend
- 3 tsp. cornstarch
- 1 tsp. vanilla extract
- ½ cup water

xxxxxxxxxxxxxxxxxxxxxxxxxxxxxxxxxxxxxxxxxxxxx

How to Cook:

Mix the stevia baking blend and cornstarch and sift them. Set aside.

Mix the vanilla extract, water and meringue powder. Beat until stiff peaks with a whisk attachment.

Add the stevia mixture and mix well.

(27) Stevia Lemonade

If you are looking for the perfect refreshing beverage, this is it. The fresh lemonade is low in calories and will give you the energy to seize your day.

Duration: 15 minutes

Serving Size: 4

List of Ingredients:

- 3 lemons
- 1 to 2 tsp. stevia
- 1 qt. water
- Ice cubes as needed

xxxxxxxxxxxxxxxxxxxxxxxxxxxxxxxxxxxxxxxxxxxx

How to Cook:

Juice the lemons and strain the seeds.

Add into a pitcher and pour the water.

Start with 1 tbsp. of the stevia and go up more until you reach the desired level of sweetness.

Serve chilled over ice cubes.

(28) Stevia Simple Syrup

This secret recipe reveals the entire process of how to make a simple syrup with stevia. Whether you want to enrich your desserts or prepare your cocktails, the syrup will be handy. Prepare it and store it in the fridge for whenever you need to add a dose of sweetness.

Duration: 15 minutes

Serving Size: 1

List of Ingredients:

- 2 tbsp. + 2 ½ tsp. stevia powder
- Pinch of salt
- 1 cup water

xxxxxxxxxxxxxxxxxxxxxxxxxxxxxxxxxxxxxxxxxxxxx

How to Cook:

Mix all the ingredients in a small pot.

Heat on medium-low. When it starts to simmer, remove it from the heat.

Let your syrup cool down and store it in the fridge.

(29) Stevia Cookie Dough

This recipe is an excellent alternative to the traditional recipe made with sugar. If you adore simple edible cookie dough, the low-calorie version will become your favorite.

Duration: 20 minutes

Serving Size: 12

List of Ingredients:

- 8 oz. softened cream cheese
- 1 softened unsalted butter stick
- 2 tsp. vanilla liquid stevia
- ¼ cup creamy peanut butter
- ½ cup sugar-free chocolate chips
- 1-2 tsp. vanilla extract

xxxxxxxxxxxxxxxxxxxxxxxxxxxxxxxxxxxxxxxxxxx

How to Cook:

Beat the cream cheese, butter, vanilla liquid stevia and peanut butter.

Add the vanilla extract and continue to beat the mixture until combined

Gently fold in the chocolate chips.

(30) Stevia Lemon Cookies

If you crave fresh citrus cookies, this recipe is the right choice for your end. The addition of lemon adds a dose of flavor, while the stevia takes calories off.

Duration: 15 minutes

Serving Size: 12

List of Ingredients:

- ¼ cup stevia
- 5 oz. unsalted butter, melted
- 1 egg
- ½ cup coconut flour
- Zest of ½ lemon
- Juice of ½ lemon

xxxxxxxxxxxxxxxxxxxxxxxxxxxxxxxxxxxxxxxxxxx

How to Cook:

Preheat the oven to 350 degrees F.

Line a baking sheet with parchment paper and grease it.

Let the butter cool down to room temperature and mix with the egg, lemon zest, lemon juice and stevia.

When the mixture is combined, add the coconut flour gradually.

Spoon the mixture on the sheet and flatten it.

Bake for 10 to 15 minutes.

About the Author

From a young age, Zoe loved being in the kitchen! More specifically, her uncle's bakery. Despite not actually working there, she would sit on the working table and watch herself get covered in flour over the next couple of hours. She also watched closely as her uncle kneaded the dough, measured out ingredients, and even decorated cakes. Even though she never tried doing it herself, she could recite the steps to most of the baked goods sold like her favorite song.

It wasn't until her 16th birthday, though, that she realized just how much she wanted to dedicate her life to making desserts too. No matter how much Zoe's mom insisted on buying a beautiful cake from a local bakery for her Sweet 16 party, Zoe wouldn't budge. She wanted to make the cake herself, and she did. Even though it wasn't the prettiest of cakes, it tasted delicious! Her whole family still remembers the flavor combo to this day: pistachio and orange cake. From there, things only got better!

After graduating from culinary school, Zoe worked in some of the finest bakeries throughout Europe. She wanted to learn from the best. Eventually, however, she decided to go back home and start her own business in Chicago, near her friends and family. That business is now one of the nicest bakeries in the city, which she has run with the help of her best friend, Lola, since 2015

Author's Afterthoughts

Hi there!

This is me trying to thank you for supporting my writing by purchasing my cookbook. I can't begin to express how much it means to me! Even though I've been doing this for quite a while now, I still love to know that people enjoy making my recipes, and I like to thank them for it personally.

You see, without you, my job would be meaningless. A cook with no one to eat their food? A cookbook author with no one to read their book? I need you to love my work to be rewarding, so do you?

One of the biggest ways to thank you for supporting me is by asking what you like or dislike most about my books. Are the recipes easy to follow? Do you think I should write more baking books, or what would you like to see more of? I will get to your suggestions for new books and improvements soon, ready to use them for my next book — so don't be shy!

THANK YOU.

ZOE MOORE

Printed in Great Britain
by Amazon